Riverbed Treasures

Selected Poems
by
Sarah Clarissa Mieras
aka saraclarissa

Photo
All photos by Sarah Clarissa Mieras
Cover photo of the Grand River
Artist headshot Lookout Park/Belknap

Grand River Poetry Collective
https://grandriverpoetrycollective.com

For Sunny and Jules

Praise For *Riverbed Treasures*

"Sarah Clarissa Mieras' *Riverbed Treasures* is a stellar book of poems. She tackles a variety of difficult subjects, ranging from the opening poem which is a paean to queer poets who made this generation's poets more free to express their thoughts, the feminist grasp of the struggle with one's sexuality and the problems of patriarchy, as well as the problem of her father's PTSD and Agent Orange which morphed her DNA per his time in Vietnam-- these all without being didactic, her empathy on display in every poem while pointing out the concerns inherent in her subjects.

There are also tender love poems, concerns for those trapped in poverty via capitalist blindness and cruelty, and surprises ranging from the long history of Native Americans on the land where our city now lies, from Hopewell mound builders to present-day Anishinaabe.

She also explores the need to complete one's own self through the tenderness of others, as in the final lines of "Me, My Body And I": "bring your finger to my skin and / steal me from / the boundaries of me, myself and I."

The book is loaded with direct activist work, always following William Carlos Williams' dictum: "go back to the people. They are the origin of every bit of life of conceivable human interest.

There's not a bad poem here—buy it! It's true to its title, a book of riverbed treasures."

— **David Cope**, author of
  - *Moonlight Rose in Blue: Collected Poems 1971-2024,*
  - *A Bridge Across the Pacific:*
   Leaves for Chen Zi'ang, Guan Yin and /Du Fu,
  - *The Correspondence of David Cope & Allen Ginsberg 1976-1996,*
  - and former Grand Rapids Poet Laureate

Praise For *Riverbed Treasures*

"*Riverbed Treasures* is a debut collection that understands the body, the land, and history as sites of injury and personal inheritance.

Sarah Clarissa Mieras writes with a steady, unflinching gaze and moves through war, queer embodiment, grief, desire, and the natural world not to resolve them, but to listen closely to what they carry.

These poems move like water over stone: patient, erosive, luminous with attention. Again and again, Mieras reveals survival as an active practice—an ongoing act of witness, care, and becoming.

What emerges is a book of hard-won beauty, grounded in the river's wisdom and animated by a voice that trusts silence as much as speech.

This is vibrant, necessary work—poetry that does not look away, and in doing so, offers us a way to stay.

Mieras's work is at its strongest when describing how passion drives the physical world in poems such as "Cyborg,""Tent Barker," and "A River Dialogue" where treasure is "lost in the murky water, / waiting to be re-discovered.""

— **Christine Stephens-Krieger**, author of
- *Love Garden at the End of the World*
- and Grand Rapids Poet Laureate 2024-2027

Praise For *Riverbed Treasures*

"Sarah Clarissa Mieras' *Riverbed Treasures* is a sourcebook — a veritable treasure chest — on what to do with essential conscientiousness of matters personal, social, political, local, universal, environmental, and more. She exemplifies how it is necessary to write and read poetry for the survival of our souls.

These poems hold stories of joys and disasters, sometimes holding joy in one hand, disaster in the other, in the same poem, illuminating complexities of life circumstances with great clarity and abundant skill with the written word.

She's a strong advocate, championing the stories of so many marginalized people with an eye for accuracy and an eye seeing art.

Mieras' book sees me, and I'm sure you will feel seen in a new way, too, upon reading it. I don't know if there's any better feeling than that.

Teeming with invention, strenuously honest, advocative, and artistic, you can feel Mieras' masterful craft in every poem in her book."

— **Neil Kaufman**, author of *Jungle Gyms for Monkey Minds*

"Sarah's debut collection of poetry traces the making of a poet shaped by survival, tenderness and defiance. Sarah writes from a place that is vulnerable, raw and unflinching.

Her poems move through pain and pleasure, longing and resilience, mapping the moments, memories, and scars that have forged her into who she is today.

Each piece invites the reader on a journey of becoming. One that transforms difference into power and lived experience into art."

— **Leslie Papp**, author of *what am i afraid of*

Praise For *Riverbed Treasures*

"*Riverbed Treasures* captures the essence of why art impacts us - a dance between the chaotic and the orderly, the meaningful and the arbitrary.

Flowing between themes, Sarah Mieras' voice both leaps off the page with integrity and grit and grows roots deep into the physical environment.

She names what is— what it means to live in this "political circus," and among an "urban smear." Mieras invites us "to open our red centered mouths / and scream into being" and to do it together, as a community.

These powerful poems are both local and cosmic, guiding us from a single moment alone and in pain to an exchange between strangers on the street and out into the connectedness of all things."

— **Camille Newsom**, author of *Purgatory Junky*

"Mieras crafts poetry with bold confidence informed by deep insights, colored by the vibrant experiences of her life. She shares her gifts with an obvious reverence for her art.

Each piece is a deeply moving experience that engages the reader long after you have left the page. Just as those stones not broken by the sometimes brutal forces of nature become beautiful testaments to the beauty of endurance, so does Mieras' debut book. It is sure to delight and inspire anyone that reads it.

This is one of those works I will return to often with the same excitement as the first time I read these power filled words, feeling a great sense of gratitude for Mieras' soulful contribution to the world."

— **Ben Snider**, Poet and member of Grand River Poetry Collective

Contents

Woman

Sex

The Poet's Ways

Humanity

Holy, Holy, Holy:
A Footnote to the Footnote of Howl

Holy, Holy, Holy
the ordinary queer prophets
pounding the keys with truth
who have for centuries laid the words
that would define
generations.

Holy Sappho
Holy Oscar Wilde
Holy Emily Dickinson
Holy Walt Whitman
Holy James Baldwin
Holy Radcliffe Hall
Holy Frank O'Hara
Holy Gertrude Stein and
Alice Toklas, too
Holy Langston Hughes
Holy W.H. Auden
Holy Audre Lorde
Holy Adrienne Rich
Holy Alice Walker
Holy Mary Oliver
Holy Andrea Gibson
Holy Renee Nicole Good
Holy, Holy, Holy
Allen Ginsberg

Holy, Holy, Holy
Holy the queer artists
swimming upstream
leaving enlightenment
for the masses in their wake.

* Dedicated to Allen Ginsberg

Currency

Empty corners curve,
leaf laden and twisting
as I canvas the neighborhood.

Every image becoming a metaphor
as my feet move past it in the visual slam of life.

The washed numb
of our isolated existence
defined by consumption
is on display in every storefront I pass.

Are we more defined by our work
or that which
we work to consume?

I drop a coin, a silver piece that is not silver,
into the cup of the man on the corner.

I have little, but he has less.

The cold round disk floats then
hits the cup's empty bottom
with a clink.

There is not much
but everything between us.

Shoe bound desire for home, I keep walking,
and I wonder
what the boundaries of
possible
could be
without currency
to define us.

American Refugees Living on the Edge

There are places like this worn brick building
known as "The 6" on the edge of every town.

Places you drive by and immediately feel sorry for anyone inside.
You can smell it from the road; bedbugs, mildew, and desperation.
It is hard to imagine what would make anyone stop and stay.

Inside, there are people who know only where they have been,
what they have survived, escaped, and endured;
not where they are going.
All of them reeking of human tragedy. Mold. Fire. Floods. Storms. Abuse.

The parking lot is filled with aged, broken down cars;
all bearing scars of accidents and incidents,
scrapes, and near misses, flat tires, and broken lights.
Like their drivers, these cars have seen some shit.

Each busted ride is filled with remnants of the tragic series of events
that culminated in someone calling this motel home.
Scattered bits of a life now lost litter the seats
telling parts of the story that brought them here.

That life now lost to the tyranny of the urgent –
to making it through each sun rise and fall intact.

American refugees of corporate greed
under-housed and unseen
forgotten and hiding, barely surviving behind crumbling walls
of cheap motels that rent by the week or the month.

I left that motel on the edge of town a while ago.
I emptied the remnants of my lost life from my car.
I made it out. I planted a new garden.
I can still smell that place on me sometimes though,
mildew, injustice, and desperation.

Numbers

I have stopped counting the days that I have been alone.
There will be more.
I write down the number of dead announced each night in a notebook.
Lives lost
now numbers on news banners
like lotto or election results.

Nothing is normal.
This is 2020.
This is COVID-19.

Motown is running out of coolers for the dead.
In L.A. families are putting their dead on ice
while they await the coroner.

Streets everywhere are empty
like apocalyptic movie sets.
Scared eyes stare over hand-sewn face masks.

I weigh interactions with other humans
on a risk scale as dire as
"Is it worth dying or killing for?"

Ritualistically
I record the numbers in my notebook
people gone.
No funeral.
No wake.
No names.
No news story.
People reduced to numbers
in a viral political circus
of failed morality.

3-23-2020:	473 U.S. dead
4-23-2020:	48,144 U.S. dead
8-28-2020:	180,000 U.S. dead
10-26-2020:	229,721 U.S. dead
3-26-2021:	555,775 U.S. dead

Will we honor them in the future?

Will the victims of COVID-19 someday
reclaim their names
like colorful patches
on an AIDS Quilt at a Pride parade?

Each square a name sewn with love.
Each square a reminder of preventable death.
Each square a life lost and remembered.

Or will forgetting that
these numbers
are names
become a necessity
for those who survive?

Update 2025:

More than 1.2 Million Americans dead
and no one is really counting anymore.

A Civilized Dance: A Museum Exhibit Opening

The dancers stand front to back
waiting to be told to move to the rhythm
the hollow pat of the drums hangs in the air.

Some twitch as nervous beads of sweat
roll in slow meter down their backs.
It is their first "museum dance"
in the worn leather moccasins.

The crowd swells thickly around them,
white faces with red painted smiles.

Tickets in hand they stand a mob of America
behind the yellow silk ropes
the museum uses to keep hands off the artifacts.

The drumming gets louder
and the breath of America draws in
to anticipate history
unraveling
in the eye-catching shine
of the dancers'
feathers, leather, and beads.

The single-file line spreads out
and
bends into a circle of feet.

Through the skylight,
the sun melts in ribbons,
casting shadows over the dancers.

It starts at the drum with the grey man.
He has done this before.
He knows it is the chant of spirit,
the fields of knowing
spreading into mouths
and curling around tongues
that are important.

It starts at the drum and catches the heels of the dancers.
It moves them in a circle.
It carries their voices,
guiding their breath and articulation.

They have become the sound.
They have become the people of the past.

The skylight grows dark and the drum STOPS.

On cue, the audience folds their programs
and flows down the stairs to the red glow
of the EXIT sign.
Some kids pound flat palms over their mouths
shouting,
"Ya. Ya. Ya. Ya. Ya."

At the exhibit,
the dancers stand alone,
behind the yellow silk ropes.

Dedicated to the Anishinaabe people.

Appendix p.84-85

An Eye Opening Slowly

I have closed my eyes to the spots of light,
the never-ending movement of people
that maps the streets in glowing pointillism.

The lack of light
has driven my sight inward
on a pilgrimage of simplicity
where I strive to be only
an eye
opening slowly
to the hand
reaching for its lashes.

When the eye opens slowly you can see.
I am you.
And you are me.
We are all the same.

And we can all see
the machine's misplaced oil
left to stain
the streets in rainbow splashes.

Straddling the yellow lines
of the street where I stand,
I am only
one human
pausing to see
the crossing of threads
through the loom
of now.

I am just one eye
opening slowly.

Choices

Capitalist towers of glass loom overhead
reflecting the lights of the city
over the river at 4 a.m.

I am writing from inside the urban smear of America.
A place where parking lots
between mini malls and warehouse stores connect cities.
The houses scattered in between.

The noise of people running from need to need
bounces off the concrete making the populace a song.

In between the constant need for consumption,
and the working to fund the consumption, the living happens.

Tapping the keys, I am connecting syllables with dreams.

I want to see light in the darkness.
I want to see beyond enduring the inevitable pains of consumption.

I want to dream new realities where
peace and love are
the new standards for margins of profit.

I want to dream a reality where kindness
not cruelty is the point.

I want to believe it is possible for us to repair
the mess we have made.

I want to believe we can heal,
one good choice
at a time.

Speaking of Revolution

Outside a Tucson cafe an unshaven man who smelled ripe
with the setting of the sun
asked me for a dollar and said,

"We know the world is turning beneath us.
Still, it is only when we stop
to witness the turning
of the sphere that we notice the
revolution."

Long after the scent of him had faded
from the hot desert air
his words bounced
like a rubber ball
in my mind.
"We. Fire.
Sphere.
Revolution."

Could we?
Could we get it together?
We the subject. We the people.

Could We finally
and forever agree
that each
We
is the We
of "We the People?"

Maybe then
the Revolution
capable of turning
the sphere
can begin.

Cardboard Protest Signs in the Capitalist Republic

The drain of apathy weighs heavy on the mind of the knowing.
The cozy comforts of ignorant bliss surround and sedate.
People won't care until their shelves are empty,
or until their neighbors are disappeared.

Until then, do what you can.
Paint your outrage at the loss of the American Dream
on a protest sign and hold it up high.
Be a catalyst of change.
Run into the green light one way of no return screaming your truth.

Jam on urban pioneers of thought viruses,
holding signs at the exit ramps and overpasses.
One protest at a time,
may you unearth the formula for resistance
that has gathered dust during times of comfort.
May you define and build the movement
strong enough to save us all
from our purchased leaders of Armageddon.

To subvert the cruelty the counter Revolution of Kindness
will be led by ordinary soldiers
upholding human decency.
Those willing to risk it all, to save us all.
May the Revolution be launched in self-published ramblings
of ordinary prophets.
Everyone can participate.
Don't buy the emptiness and angst
cross marketed for our consumption, co-option and silence.
Don't eat the screen driven emptiness
designed to numb your mind and secure your cooperation.

Define yourself.   Probe the lies.   See with your heart.
Be a catalyst of change.
Run into the green light one way of no return screaming your truth.

Tent Barker

I

My father was a tent barker
for the Fat Lady at a carnival freak show.

The lost boy with an impish grin, he was an expected
quirky part of the show experience.

At 13-years-old he moved with the carnival from town to town.
His voice a lashing lasso
that filled Baby Flo Johnson's Tent
one fat joke at a time.

With character, one-liners and flattery
he ushered the house full so the show could begin
again and again.

II

"Gates!"
"Gates!"
"Gates!"

A voice calls out on the radio clipped to my shirt.
The information barely beats the stampede of feet
moving the ether around me,
all rushing for the sound that drew them here.
It is showtime.
And I
am now
an absolutely hyperbolic nearly operatic
human navigational device
to herd and safe keep the faceless masses
craven for tonight's flavor of artistic catharsis.

The crowd grows thicker,
and I grow louder.

I force my voice
to be heard.
I morph my banter
to jive
with each group
on
its unique wavelength.

As I massage the crowd
into the house
I realize
how natural this is for me.

That runaway teen,
the little brother
to the circus salesman,
that
carnival tent barker
for Lady Flo,
taught me
everything I know.
And not all
of the show
happens on stage.

Appendix p.84-85

Numb

Part I: 1999

Click here to browse and surf
the realm of digital media mania.
Everyone with a connection can broadcast.
Click. Click. Click.
It's the new background noise of the American Dream.
Click here for the next installment
of patriarchal capitalist propaganda for the masses.
Click. View. Surf. Browse.
Until your orbs are numb.

Numb to the real beyond the glow of the screen.
Numb to the unplugged, wandering on the street beneath you.
Everyone is everywhere, but no one is here.
Everyone can broadcast, but no one is listening.

Part II: 2025

The data of our hours,
fractured syllables
misplaced words
ones and zeros
letters and numbers flying through space
scatter in the air waves.

One. One. Zero. Zero. Zero. One.

It is the data footprint of our hours,
our identity in the data-verse.

We are the product and the consumer.
In bits and bites the algorithm records the movement of our hours.

In and out our data moves
a digital breath feeding the binary river of our self consumption.

Cyborg

Plugged in and scrolling
I came to know without warning
that multiple unaccredited sources agree:
I can now
subjectively and medically
identify as a "cyborg."

Born broken,
my crumbling spine
now updated
and upgraded,
a tower of
steel,
screws,
and titanium rods.
I am now part human, part machine.

Strangers hold me up now.
Angel's wings made of donor bone
flank and brace my new spine.

My backbone is now sturdy,
rebuilt with ground bits of random skeletons
mixed with plastic
to hold the screws,
and rods, and cages.

Fragments
of many
now
make up my
one
machine.

Dedicated to all organ donors.

War

A Veteran's Holiday

It is the same each year.
He lies on the floor with iron fists, a tight jaw,
and distant dark brown eyes.

He takes shelter beneath the kitchen table.

"I killed a man!" he yells.
"I watched him bleed, and then I crawled away."

An explosion shakes the house,
followed by the hiss of the fireworks
spinning colors in the sky.

"Make it stop!" he cries out.

But the fireworks keep flying.

And his children say,
"Daddy, Daddy, it's okay.
You don't have to go to war today."

Stains of War

It stains my hands
like the Lady Macbeth I am running mad
down the hallways in my mind.

I did not spill the blood
but it stains me anyway.
No war ever ends.

No destruction unleashed,
no blood spilled, bombs dropped, or toxin dispersed
have an expiration date.

No war ever ends.

Cities. Places. Order. They may return.
But the stains of war remain.

With time stains fade to blurry family stories of service and bravery.
Still no warrior gains the title without shedding blood.
Each medal proof of kill to the god of Country.

I can't get it off my hands or out of my mind,
all of the blood spilled, staining layers of time.

The actions of war haunt
the aggressors
and the victims alike
for generations.

So, what generation will it be
who dares to decide
the pain
and financial gain
are not worth
the stain?

Duck

My grandfather in his death bed,
one foot blackened, writhing in a diaper
and calling for his mother,
found comfort in the music of his childhood.

To soothe him I played Bizet's *Carmen,*
Wagner's *The Flying Dutchman* and
the Benedictine Monks' Catholic Mass in Latin.

His moaning would pivot to a hum, his rock joining
time with the rise of the strings and the boom of Wagner's waves.

Sitting on his stool in the kitchen,
I am surrounded by the sturdy cabinets he built,
and the children he broke.

They can feel it coming. The loss of fuel for their anger.

I enter his room, he moans, "Duck!"
I drop to the floor and look for imaginary planes overhead.
In these last days phrases like
"Duck boys I can hear the planes!" and
"Everybody duck!" have become routine.

A child of the Great Depression,
at five he walked with a red wagon
to stand in line for scraps at the butcher shop.
A head was always the goal.

Still, it was the horrors of World War II
where he fought as a patriotic boy
that would haunt
his unraveling mind
as death crawled up his body
from his feet to his heart.

Collateral Unicorn

"Well, aren't you just the Collateral Unicorn,"
a guy at the Veterans Administration said over a scratchy phone line.
"There aren't many of you left anymore."

I hung up and felt the place at the base of my spine
that never stops aching.
The place where the hole in bone is called Spina Bifida.

A byproduct of chemical warfare
I am an all-American-made Genetically Modified Organism,
a human GMO.

I am the child of the 19-year-old boy
who painted peace signs on warheads
at Naval Detachment Cat Lo, Vietnam, 1968.

I am the daughter of the bare chested sailor
who sprayed poison by hand
onto the riverbanks of the Mekong Delta,
and then lit it on fire,
all before he was old enough to vote.

I am the daughter of a man who survived the Vietnam War
only to carry home its most egregious weapon in his DNA.

No one expected the boy to live,
so what the poison would do the boy,
his children, or their children was not equated or actuated.
The calculation wasn't profitable.

Still, here I am.
A mythical creature,
a Collateral Unicorn;
one not expected to survive.

I am spreadsheet anomaly
on the post-war expense side.

My code shifted inside my father's sack.
I was born with a broken back.

I write so there is a record that I exist.
That we exist.
We, the genetically altered children of chemical warfare.

I am just one of many.
All born of seeds
soaked in dioxin and sunshine in Vietnam.
Our bodies altered by a poison that promised to
"kill to the root,"
so plants could never set seed again.

2-4-5-T
the chemical signature
for the method of war;
the herbicide Agent Orange.

2-4-5-T
The signature of my deformities;
my enemy, and my descriptor.

Agent Orange,
made by the Red, White, and Blue.
A toxic gift
from the chemical companies
to my Dad, to me and you,
and the generation after us,
and the one after them,
and the next one too.

Dedicated to all generations of Agent Orange survivors.

Appendix p.84-85

Ancient Waters

Getting Caught Up

The hum of the one current that is all currents runs over the rocks and lulls me.
It never stops.
I toss some sticks, tiny twigs that winter's weight shook
from the branches of this maple where I lean.

Clinging to the eroded bank, it dangles thirsty roots in the clear water.
Balancing on the edge, its branches reach into the clouds.

These twigs, the children that could not stay when the winds came.
I toss them into the stream to watch the current hold up their twisted bodies.
The stream doesn't stop with their weight.
It pushes into the next open stretch
where the sun can see herself in rippled perfection.

These carcasses, these tiny sticks,
they ride the stream.
coasting on the current that is always there.

The roots catch hold of them, and one by one
they pile upon each other.
These twigs, they damn themselves.

Held in the roots they tread, simply staying afloat.
Their bodies tangled together,
they don't care that the unceasing current has ceased to carry them.

The current keeps pushing on, curling around the bends, and
stretching out in the long spaces where the sun bathes.

As I drop the broken into the ripples
I see my shadow stretched over the water
and realize
I too have been swept up in the current and
damned up in my roots.

A River Dialogue

Casting shadows like piano keys on the bronze water,
the trees
      SLIDE
           along the bank,
                shuffling
                    like prisoners
                          towards execution.
I watch as they wade into the river.

As a kid, fishing out of the back of a Volare with my Dad,
hatch-back up, tires sinking into the sand bar,
we baited hooks to the White Album,
contemplating the status of Bungalow Bill.

Waiting for a tug on a line,
I wandered the sand bars
hunting for riverbed treasures.
I filled my pockets with wet bits of history
lost beneath the brown water:
clam shells, rusted bits of things unknown,
broken shell buttons, smooth pieces of glass and rocks.
All once things now just bits
lost in the current.

One Sunday, Dad took us for a drive along the river
to see the Indian Mounds.

He thought we should know where they were.

I told him my teacher showed them to us
in the park, outside the museum downtown.

He explained those were fake mounds to fool people.
Most of the real ones, he said, were destroyed.
The ones that survived, he explained, are harder to find.

Trees folded over the bumpy old road
that sputtered with creaking oil rigs.

When we arrived,
there was a fence around the Mounds.
I asked if they were trying to keep us out,
or the dead Indians inside.

Mom just bowed her head,
lit a cigarette and said,
"Either way, they are behind the fence."

Now seated beneath a highway overpass
near those same mysterious Mounds,
people moving around me one tire turn at a time
I feel a tug
like I am the fish on the line this time.

My dad grew up on this river. His dad grew up on this river.
I grew up on this river.
All of us casting into the shadows of Devil's Elbow for the big catch.

The reel is turning.
I am on the hook now.
Turn by turn I am slowly becoming
part of the current
of this ancient place.
Part of this ever eroding tradition,
another banged up riverbed treasure
lost in the murky water,
waiting to be re-discovered.

* Dedicated to my parents, and all of my Grand River ancestors.

Appendix p.84-85

Loon Lake Mother

We slip like
blades through the lake.
We await the Loon.
All is evergreen along the shore,
the spiky reflection
of needled wood
bounces off the absolutely
clear water.

We are in the water
in the shadow of the green,
naked with our swollen bellies
and heavy breasts.

Our hearts the only human drums
in this stretch of liquid and sky.

We wait
for the high mournful calls of the Loon
to echo through the trees
like women singing in the open breeze.

The afternoon licks our nakedness.

We hear something shuffling,
rock healed through the green towards us.
We stiffen and wrestle back fear.

Could it be the Loon we came for, another camper,
or is it a wood sprite,
a blend of flesh and green?

We hear twigs crack
the sound of ferns scraping on thighs.
Ivory wisps of hair part the trees and her form becomes.

She wears a black sack dress
and necklace of pearls
her snowy hair tangles in the breeze.

She with her rights to this land.
She with her shadowy shape.
She who rubs the belly of the Earth to ease its pain.
She who has shown herself to us.
She who knows the secret life
and understands the seed pulse of the forest.
She who was not born in the concrete masses.
She whose pulse is the rhythm of the lake.
Loon Lake.
We move to touch her, to speak to her,
to uncover her secrets.
But she is gone.

We are naked on the shore
the sun evaporating the lake
from our bodies
when a shadow passes overhead.

Then, we hear it –
the cry of the Loon.
It tears open the sky
and we watch
as a stretch of feathers
casts shadows
and pearls
through the trees
while
crying like women
singing in the open breeze.

The S Curve: An Ancient Highway in the Sky

Like an S it curves in the sky above the river.
This highway in the sky is an ancient transfer point.

It snakes like an S
above the current that gives this City its name.

Concrete walls and engineering constrain
the water that flows beneath.

To the west there is the sprawling flatness
where the ancient earthen Mounds
were destroyed in the 1850s.

The action but not its meaning
recorded when men of industry
drowned and buried
the ancient places to build
new foundations.

To the east are rolling hills adorned with boulders
and Belknap Hill hangs over the river
its platformed pyramid peak facing the setting sun.

It curves like an S
through the immigrant-built steeples
that stand like watchmen of bygone times,
their gold, copper, and leaded glass
glistening points on the skyline.

The S Curve, a winding ancient transfer point in the sky.

Here at these flowing waters
people have changed lanes and chosen new paths
for thousands of years.

In the shadow of the S Curve,
out of sight, tucked into a parking lot,
a historical marker memorializes
a 3000-year-old-city

The sign says this ancient place
was called Baw-Wa-Ting.

A city as old as the pyramids
along the Grand River
in the middle of Michigan,
an island framed by fresh water seas.

Like a snake suspended it
curves in the clouds
and winds together
history and future,
a sacred turning point in the sky
hovering over ancient waters.

Our roads built on their roads.
Their roads built on the roads of those before them.
Those roads on those of those before them.

Baw-Wa-Ting
an ancient transfer point
long destroyed
but not forgotten.

* Dedicated to the Hopewell Mound Builders,
and to all of the people who have called Grand Rapids, or Baw-Wa-Ting home.

Appendix p.84-85

Woman

Becoming

Tonight I awake to my dying.
I rise from stiff white cotton.

I pull myself from the spot,
a shadow of my insides, dark and coagulated.

I wrap my sheet around me
and wander into the yard,
dripping a path of myself onto the lawn
to glisten like sequins on the grass.

I go to the oak.
Alone
I shed-the-little-girl
and
her bloodied cotton sheet.

From behind a cloud the moon comes down.
She cuts through the tall grass.
She touches my belly, rubbing my new sharp pain.
She cleans my legs with the autumn dead
that lay silent and brown at my feet.

Inside my head she pounds her rhythm,
our rhythm,
while I,
swelling and aching,
dripping and pounding,
I have died
to become woman.

Growing Into the Hazards

Picture the scene:
There are three crones seated at a table in a kitchen.
It is a comfortable 1920s Sears kit home
on the west side of the river
in an average mid-sized town, built on native land,
with scars rising from the tracks of carriages,
and trains that hauled lumber to the river.

Behind the shadow of a door there is a small girl
listening to the crones.

Her face has gone pale.

"It happens."
"So it does."
"So sad."
"She is so young."
"Was."
"Yes, was."
"Where did it happen?"
"The news said she was riding home from school."
"Alone?"
"Yes, it seems so."
"Perhaps she should have taken the bus."
"It matters little now what she should have done!"
"Yes, you're right."
"I doubt these things can be prevented."
"Think of her mother, that poor woman."

Listening at the edge of the room
behind the shadow of the door
that small girl
is no longer small.
She has now grown
into the hazards of being a woman.

Understanding the Gap

When they showed us the film in class
some boys giggled,
but most everybody stared really hard

at her
at her hole
at its head
trying
to
get
through
the
gap.

I closed my eyes
and clenched my teeth
as the camera zoomed in
to focus on her face,
her sweat,
her mouth twisted in pain.

When it finally popped out
everyone laughed except me.
.
I sat, stiff backed,
my hands between my legs
squeezing my thighs
around
the gap.

Between Your Legs

To be a woman
is to know
that you possess
the most
legislated
and
controlled object
on the planet
between your legs.

The Bondage of Sex

My mother in her chair
the arms worn raw,
the table spotted with white tubes
red at the ends like her lips,
stares off into the distance.

Watching my brother and me play,
she knows she will need to make me tough.

She knows our futures will not be as equal
as two children playing side by side.

Is "equality" just an empty
patriarchal myth,
a phallic upward bound idealism
coached to little girls
and the lesser-thans
to give them hope
that they can move up?

I have always wanted
to be
bonded
branded
defined
categorized
by more
than what
is between my legs.

Reclaiming the Sisterhood

My Sisters,
at night when the world is sleeping,
I hear you, like me, your faces pushed into pillows weeping.
It is dark where we lie, hold ourselves and sigh.

All of us crying for our rights
as human beings
to supersede our physicality
as bodies with vaginas and wombs.

It is time to see what is common among us
not
what is different.

It is time to
reclaim the sisterhood.
It is time to raise feminism from the ashes of complacency.

It is time for us to fight.
Fight like our lives depend
on the self governance of our bodies,
because they do.

Despite Our Adjectives

I am just a woman.
Men have told me so.

When I was young,
they said I was just a girl.

Now that I'm older
the adjectives have multiplied.

I am just a woman.

Just a single woman.

Just a childless woman.

Just a nasty woman.

Just a cat woman.

Just a queer woman.

Just a disabled woman.

Just a "fill in the blank" woman.

Separated and segregated
into the buckets of our dissent,
it is the last word that
must bind us together like a spider's web.

We are all women.

And we are all at war
for our self control in a patriarchy
no matter what our adjectives are.

Calling the Goddess of Justice for Women

Vocatio O Fortuna Muliebris

May the giver of good fortune to women
come and watch over us.

May she guard the words cast in ruby spirals
letters coagulated on pages
penned by the palms of women
imprisoned by their sex.

May she inspire in us
the sense that all is strange
except that which we share
and do not choose,
our sex.

May good fortune and justice protect all women.
May her power fold in the walls,
and lift the ceiling,
revealing the openness of our minds
to the words of our sisters,
revealing the openness of our minds
to all of the facets
of being entailed
in occupying
the body
of a woman.

Lady Liberty we need you now
to even the scales.

Vocatio O Fortuna Muliebris

Appendix p.84-85

Playing the Crease

It's late again and I am the only one awake
watching the snow fall in patterns
on the parked cars along the curb.

My breath birthing clouds under the streetlights,
my fingers play the crease of a paper in my pocket.
Folded twice, it holds the number
of a body whose place
in the dichotomies of gender
has been lost.

A body driven underground,
broad shouldered, never one for skirts,
a classic tomboy.

But she, no longer feeling so much a she,
has crossed,
in thick soled black boots
the lines between she and he,
solidifying a position somewhere inside
the undefined middle.

A canary yellow cab speeds by
tossing slush and grit into my face.

The cold sting pulls me
from the questions
of who
she is
now
and
who they
will
become.

She Belly

She is resisting the hunger to starve the sides
of her that cannot fit
into the allotted space.

Her hands rest
on her stomach's round hump.
She's tried to starve it off,
and
now she has become the hunger.

She has become
the hump
the celluloid lump,
that reminds mothers to buy "fat free."

She is the poster girl
for obesity
and shame,
shame of womanly bodies full and round,
shame of size
and influence.

She is the woman who cannot fit
within the space allowed,
her sides flowing over
the arms of chairs.
She has exceeded
the limits of personal
space, circumference, and width.

Chubby, pleasantly plump, fat, large, obese, bigger, plus-sized,
overweight, big-boned, husky and heavy;

all adjectives crafted to describe the visual dimensions of her difference.

Imagine now
a big, beautiful,
naked FAT woman
stands before a mirror.
She cradles the hump
of her stomach in her arms.

She blames it for her isolation.
She loves it
for its full moon curve
of flesh,
its warmth,
its pillow-like softness,
and
the protection
it gives her.

Turning in the mirror,
examining
her fullness
she embraces
the
odd truth
that this
roundness
that has
never left
is
the
most
authentic
part
of her.

Sex

An Explication of Jouir

Spring rises through waddle worthy
pools of melting snow
displaying the buried ecstasy of green
spreading across the hills in our yard.

Clear azure
hangs like a backdrop
above the smoking chimneys
and brick
that frame the window
where we lie naked
on sweat-stained sheets
fondling the explication of jouir.

Appendix p.84-85

A Semantic Journey of "I Love You"

Watching the January cold crawl up
the steamy window in a web of frost
I feel the warmth of your palm cupping my breast.
I breathe in.

With tongue in ear you moan
for the release
of words
long locked
in the feeling
of lying naked and numb
in the frost.

Somehow
within the pause
of hand over flesh
the meaning of all this emotion
is reduced to merely
a matter of semantics.

And three worn words
rise like a white picket fence
and move over the points of your teeth.

"I love you."

The Space Between December Hands

Headlight smear of moments measure an eve spent wandering
the streets in an early December fog.

I stood alone watching the smoke rise into swirled patterns above my head as the
clock on the bank at the corner of Division and Liberty hit midnight.

Liberty Square was empty like my palm.

1:00
Could my hand have not moved slowly across the room to slip from your
shoulder the white cotton of your shirt?

2:27
Reclining on three navy pillows,
You a mane falling in curls.
The rise of breasts. The opening of lips.
The sound of your breath blending with the pulse of the t.v. screen.

3:37
I am obsessed with the moment, with the place,
with the spread of time moving us from scene to scene over bricks
and through astrology in our urban shoes, thick-soled and dirty,
crossing cement squares, spotted black with chewing gum.

4:47
The street is void of noise.
A nude body passes across an ignited shade.
It draws your eyes as we stand at the door.
Now our eyes are open to the space drawing closer between us.

5:57
Alone again, watching the smoke rise from my fingertips,
I crush the tar and breathe through these moments now gone,
bypassed along the fault line of touch.

Broken

Sometimes the center
opens
and I   can see
where   you
broke   yourself
at 13,   and I
know   why
you   whimper
in your sleep.

Wanting

Woman
with
your sea blue eyes
that change with the clouds
please
do dare to lean
lean
forward
with open lips
to cross the lines
between
us
and
kiss me,
kiss me
just once.

Utopia

Two flesh forms
hardly secure in perfection
slip
into the white light
that tumbles onto
the worn cotton sheet
from
the hummin' bulb
hanging beyond
the window pane.

Me, My Body, and I

Often, in the morning
it is hard to ascertain
the difference between the clouds
and the branches of the trees,
the body of their mass leaning into the breeze.
The branches all covered
in glistening winter
that came by surprise
to layer the green with white.

I've spent too much time talking to
and about my body,
and not enough time living in it.

Temple of the mind, body born mortality,
shell-shocked, and crumbling,
where do you go when the mind is on fire
and the body is withering away?

Can you reach me?
Just touch me.
Bring your finger to my skin.

Touch me and awaken
the shell of misfiring synapses
that is the broken body of me.

Awaken the me inside the I.

Just bring your finger to my skin,
and take away the pain,
bring your finger to my skin and
steal me from
the boundaries of me, myself and I.

You Me in the Morning Passion Jungle

I feel the slide of your breast
across my belly
all round and mounded.
You me
the floating sun of morning orange
slipping liquid talons
through the blinds.
You me
the arching
diving pushing
and thrusting
of wet places
meeting and sliding
the long length of the exhale.
You me
blended rounds
of flesh splayed out
when the calmness of body
has come.
You me
spreading softly ruffled syllables
over these borrowed apartment walls.

Saxophonic Romance

Light curves smooth over the sax
while nimble fingers turn buttons and breath into screams.
It is alive and each note blows pure emotion all over the place.

People, what's your rush can't you hear that jazz?
Can't you feel it.
Everybody's walkin' so fast.
I'm going to Arizona.
I'm gonna drive there fast
and then walk slow heading no where with purpose.
The Beats are all gone.
JackAllenWilliamLawrence all gone.
Their words block letters on white pages
bound in books that hold the secrets of being a good human.

Look up and see the stars reflecting off the glass ceiling'd cubicles.
The sky is a phallic stretch of capitalism in rebar and lights.
Stars.
Headlights.
Streetlights.
From this hill the city is the Milky Way,
each house a glowing like a star
on a map of the community constellation.

Can you hear that?
The Sax is a lonely child screaming for attention.
Can you dig it?
Can you feel that Saxophonic love lick your ears?
Can you feel it raise the skin on your arms?

I stopped wearing a watch, but I know you're late.
But for the saxophonic rush of love
that is you in my sight,
I will wait all night.

Front Row Frisson

A half moon hangs over pink streaks of a wildfire smoke sunset
as the stage lights fire up bright.
I drove across state lines for this,
to stand next to a stranger
and move in time with skin pricking sound.

I ride the sound waves from the musician's fingers,
electrified by the amps and speakers
it bounces, bends and flows off the bodies that surround me.

Each of our frequencies change the shape of the wave.

The hair rises on my arms
and the chill spreads like a prickly wave from limb to limb.

I am a junkie for this.
The rush. The flow.
The endorphin dump
of riding frisson in the front row.

I can't get here alone.
I need help to raise the skin on my arms and fly.
I need the vibrations of a thousand souls moving in time
connected note by note
to help me leave gravity behind.

The sound waves move through me one chord at a time.
Each progression igniting chills.

Under the glow of the stage lights in the front row,
I ride skin gasm after skin gasm.

We all need the world to stop sometimes
even if just for the length of a song.

Sweaty and dancing, my limbs flopping,
I become the wave of sound.

Like minds conducting from the front row
our fingers in the air we trace the songs flow.

We are all one
as we bounce to the sound
arms in the sky.
And in that moment of collective ecstasy
there is nothing else.

Yeah, I ride that frisson buzz.
I sound surf with strangers.
I get happily lost lost in the beat
of the prick
of skin
and jump of joy
that is the magic of frisson
in the front row.
That is,
until the end of the show,
when my broken body settles back into its place.

Without the sound to surround me
and scatter
my scrambled neurons
the hairs on my legs and arms fall,
and I become
the rhythm
of my own pain again.

Appendix p.84-85

Androgyny

The slide of denim over concrete.
I passed you on a gray
DoNothingDay,
when it didn't matter
that the space between the zenith
and the tar was blank.

When it didn't matter
whose denim strapped ass
I was rounding out with my eyes.

You had a look,
a definite James Dean KindOf slouch,
in a
Marilyn Monroe
KindOfWay

At 25 miles per hour
I wheeled through
a frame of your life.

At 25 miles per hour,
I fashioned the thought
of slinging my hand
into your back pocket
as we strolled along
in our faded Levi's and leather.

All hushed you would call me, "baby."
And I would call you?

At 25 miles per hour
I juggled your identity
and ambiguity.

The FemmeMasc way
your lines stop and turn,
blending into shape.

At 25 miles per hour
I dug the
AnyKindOfWay
you prop yourself up
on the binary
concretes
of sexuality,
an
AnywayYouGoKind
of player.

At 25 miles per hour
I wheeled through a frame of your life.

You would call me, "baby."
And I would call you:

ANDROGYNY

A two-headed-beast
of titillation.

At 25 miles per hour
you are a slow grind
on the
concrete
inside
my mind.

The Poet's Ways

Westing: A Kerouacian Journey

Holed up in the 106 degree melt of Arizona at the end of June,
I press into the glass between me and a thousand lights.
It is the hotel's courtesy slice of locality.
We are Westing
to the sound of worn tires turning over cracked black tar,
the sun melting our skin like cheap candles.
We are looking for freedom;
that mythological beast that everybody thinks
everybody else has already found.
Freedom.

There is nothing in this room that knows only travelers
to remind me of home
except the rhythm of your breath and
the lines of your body beneath the sheet.

We are Westing.
Driving the Navajo Highway in the noon heat of June.
Death without dying.
Rebirth. Enlightenment.
We are Westing, "On the Road," like Jack Kerouac.

Poets are a strange breed striving to
make art from the waste of everyday language.
When I am dead, maybe I will watch the reruns of my life,
like a made-for-tv-movie.
Maybe then I will understand this thirst
to break in my teeth on the raw miles of states
marked by passing white lines
running westward through the desert toward the sea.

This is my Westward journey, "On the Road."
This string of words melting through a motel pen
stories above the hot yellow brick of Phoenix
while my lover naps.

Modern Lady of Shalott

From here I type the world into paragraphs
of Kodak moments.
People rushing.
The sound of tires coming and going
over tar makes a hum.

One story above the tick tock precision
of passing people
I am imprisoned, clicking my keyboard.
Trapped by verse like a modern Lady of Shalott
I write stories of other's lifes.

Click
tappity, tap, tap, tap, tappity, tap, tap.
Click

Hot rubber turns beneath my window.
Everyone is on the move.
Me, I am bound to pound the keys and write.

I am trapped
by visions of letters
making words
that become
lines
in an unending poem.

Alone
I weave words
from my two-story
typewriter tenement tower
as Camelot lives
beneath my window pane.

Appendix p.84-85

Poetic Litter of Coffee Stains

Coffee stains dot the poet's litter
strewn across the table.
The worn wood pedestal strains
to hold weight of the verse,
all of it wet with hyperbole and metaphor.
Each scrap of paper stained
with the kind of emotion
that's simply too raw
to exist
outside
of a poem.
The esteemed poet and professor,
the young and aspiring writer,
seated in a cafe window.
Heads bent over latte steam and scribbled diatribes,
they sort coffee stains for a pearl.
Reading. Writing. Crafting. Discussing.
The sun moves.
Cars whizz by the Kava House.
The lattes empty and
one by one
the words begin
to assemble
and transform
into something beyond
the boundaries
of their letters.
And when it is the lines
not the lattes
that linger on their tongues,
the Professor swallows hard and says,
"That, that is when you know it is a poem."

For Miriam Pederson, who gave the precious gift of her time to so many young poets.

Voices from the Outside

In my fantasy we are all veins pumping meaning into the open urban smear of
disillusioned America.
Bodies sliding tongues over concrete shadows
leaving wet trails of thought
and emotion on the brick.

The time for silence has passed.
The "unprecedented"
has presently
presidentially
happened
again and again.

So now is the time to open our red centered mouths
and scream into being
new paths of hope and peace
with new words,
erasing the norms
of this new bleak
screen-driven world
fueled by the machines of war
and
the worst of human inclinations.

In the poet's eye every image is an allusion to a moment in time
long passed and traveled by another literary mind.

Listen in between the sounds of everyday madness.
There is a rumble of voices along the edge,
from people who live outside the lines.

For generations there have been voices rumbling outside
the web of train tracks, air strips, factories, high-rises,
suburbs, smoke stacks, and un-ending wars.

Screams from the mouths of sisters and brothers
who see the world differently.

Ignoring the melting pot fantasy
of the white picket fence,
20th century poets and prophets heard it.

Gertrude heard it, hosting Picasso and Hemingway
for her wife's special brownies in her Parisian Salon.

And Gertrude's dear Alice heard it,
as she crouched over the worn black keys of the typewriter,
immortalizing the words
penned by the body she was muse to.

A voice is a voice is a voice.

Jack' n Allen 'n Ferlinghetti 'n Burroughs heard it.
Ginsberg heard it.
Patti hears it, works it, and lives it.
Dylan sings it.

The energy from outsider voices is ever changing and ever present.

As we all struggle,
may those accustomed to the fight
- the outsiders -
step forward and spark
the fire
that
shakes awake
a disillusioned
America.

Appendix

Agent Orange:
Is an herbicide defoliant used by the U.S. Military during the Korean and Vietnam wars. More than 11.2 million gallons was sprayed in Vietnam between 1965 and 1971. Exposure to Agent Orange is linked to genetic health issues that span generations.

Agent Orange and Spina Bifida:
The Veterans Administration recognizes Spina Bifida as a second generation birth defect due to Agent Orange. In 2025, Sarah is one of an estimated 1,100 survivors in the Spina Bifida Program for Children of Vietnam Veterans.

Ah-Nab-Awen Tribute Mounds:
Landscaped replica mounds in Ah-Nab-Awen Park, outside the Gerald R.Ford Presidential Museum, represent more than 50 Earthwork Mounds which were destroyed on the west side of the Grand River in the 1850s to build modern day Grand Rapids, Michigan.

Anishinaabe:
The Ojibwe word used to describe the Indigenous peoples from multiple Tribes that occupied the Great Lakes Region.

Baw-Wa-Ting:
Ojibwe word for "at the rapids."

Baw-Wa-Ting Historical Marker:
The Historical Marker for Baw-Wa-Ting is located in a Grand Valley State University parking lot located on the southwest side of the Fulton Street Bridge in Grand Rapids, Michigan. The Historical Marker is located near where more than 3000 year old artifacts were found in 1999 during re-construction of the 131 S Curve.

Frisson:
The sensation of chills or hair standing on end in response to an artistic experience. The body's physical response to the art, usually music, triggers pleasurable sensations in the brain and releases dopamine. A skin orgasm or an aesthetic chill are colloquial terms for the experience.

Jouir:
A French slang term for an orgasm.

Lady of Shalott:
A reference to a 19th century Alfred Tennyson poem, and a painting by John William Waterhouse in which a woman is stuck weaving a tapestry from reflections of others passing her by in a mirror.

Mounds:
A colloquial term used to describe the Earthworks of the Hopewell People. Some, but not all Earthworks were used for burials. It is estimated that the Hopewell culture thrived along the riverbanks of modern day Grand Rapids more than 2000-years-ago. The only recognized surviving Mounds in Grand Rapids are the Norton Mound Group, located on private land near Millennium Park. The Grand Rapids Public Museum has oversight of the Norton Mound Group.

S-Curve:
The name of a dangerous S shaped highway interchange located in Grand Rapids, Michigan above the Grand River. In 1999 more than 3000 year old artifacts were found during re-construction of the 131 S Curve.

Tent Barker:
A circus or trade term for the loud, charismatic and over-the-top salesperson located outside of a show using banter to bring people into the seats.

Vocatio O Fortuna Muliebris:
Latin for "calling Fortuna Muliebris," who was the Roman Goddess of good fortune and fate for women. Today her likeness is represented in the American image and qualities of "Lady Liberty."

Acknowledgments and Thanks

This collection of poems would not have been possible without the support of the following people to whom I express my deepest gratitude:

Christine and Scott Stephens-Krieger, founders of the Grand River Poetry Collective, for without their dreams, guidance and inspiration this book would not exist. Thank you both for seeing me long before I saw myself.

All of the members of the Grand River Poetry Collective, especially:
David Cope, Neil Kaufman, Camille Newsom, Leslie Papp, Matt Spade,
Ben Snider, Melissa Wray, Donna Munro, R.R. Tavarez, G.F. Korreck,
Shayna Marie, Barbara Saunier.

The teachers who taught me to write and encouraged me to never stop:
Sister Pearl Mary, Stephen Hoyle, Carole Steele, and Miriam Pederson.

Mom for letting me read anything I could decipher from her bookshelves.
Dad for years spent casting stories exploring the Grand River as his Bowman.
Uncle Cary for my first camera.

Ryan Thomas for decades of artistic enthusiasm and inspiration one day at a time.
For encouragement from his helm on the Bering Sea, Captain Brian Steller.

Kelly Weed, J.D. Blue, Lori, Sondra and Kelly for years of support.

Alice for teaching me to breathe when logic and proportion had fallen dead.

Mary for listening, believing and empowering.

Publishing Acknowledgements
Poems included in this collection have been previously published,
in whole or part in:
"The Sampler," issues VI, VII, VIII and IX,
"Cellar Roots," the "Lit Journal," "The Pendragon,"
"New Attitude," and the online journal "The River."

About the Author

Sarah Clarissa Mieras
aka saraclarissa

A 20th century newspaper journalist, photographer and editor, Mieras also pounded the keys as the Director of Communications for a professional opera company and as the Director of Marketing for a historic music venue built by women.

A graduate of Aquinas College, she values service and has organized, worked as crew and volunteered at festivals, concerts, Pride events and non profit music venues for more than 30 years.

She is a second generation Agent Orange survivor and is part of the Spina Bifida program for children of Vietnam Veterans.

Mieras has performed her poetry since the early 1990s. Her writing has earned awards in multiple genres from graduate research to investigative journalism.

An avid gardener, rock hound, volunteer, songwriter, activist, tree hugger and music lover, she currently resides in her hometown of Grand Rapids, Michigan.

Riverbed Treasures is her first book of poetry.

www.ingramcontent.com/pod-product-compliance
Lightning Source LLC
Chambersburg PA
CBHW051231120626
46547CB00013B/1601